THE
SECRET
VISITOR'S
GUIDE

Other works by
Ken Waldman

Poetry:

Nome Poems
(West End Press, 2000)

To Live on this Earth
(West End Press, 2002)

And Shadow Remained
(Pavement Saw Press, 2006)

Recordings:

A Week in Eek

Burnt Down House

Music Party

All Originals, All Traditionals

Fiddling Poets on Parade

THE SECRET VISITOR'S GUIDE

KEN WALDMAN

San Antonio, Texas
2006

The Secret Visitor's Guide © 2006
by Wings Press for Ken Waldman

Cover painting, "Broken Plane"
© 2002 by Don Van Radke

Author photo by Kate Wool.

First Edition

ISBN: 0-916727-26-2 (paperback original)

Wings Press
627 E. Guenther
San Antonio, Texas 78210
Phone/fax: (210) 271-7805

On-line catalogue and ordering:
www.wingspress.com

Contents

III

IV

V

VI

Grateful acknowledgment is made to the editors of the following journals in which some of these poems, or versions of these poems, first appeared, or will appear:

20 Pounds of Headlights: "Snow Angels"
A Hundred Poets Against the War: "Where There's War"
Appalachia: "Women's Bay, Kodiak"
Beloit Poetry Journal: "The Further Work"
Borderlands: "40th Birthday"
Cape Rock: "The Galax Sound"
Chariton Review: "Bill Stafford"
Comstock Review: "Minor Head Injury"
Gamut: "At the Intersection of Market and Vine"
Gargoyle: "The Violinmakers"
Ice-Floe: "High Tide" "Stebbins Trip"
Interim: "Fairbanks, 3 A.M."
Midwest Quarterly: "Gardeners, or Not"
Montserrat Review: "Fiddle and Banjo"
Plainsongs: "Coyote Pantoum"
Potato Eyes: "Farming"
Puerto del Sol: "Laura Louise"
Rio Grande Review: "Inupiat Country"
Slightly West: "But For Wilderness"
Solo: "Dawn Coyote"
Sow's Ear Poetry Review: "Light Tonight"
Sulphur River Review: "Noah's Half Sister"
Tar River Poetry: "Difficulty's Last Stand"
To Live on this Earth (West End Press): "September 11, 2001"
Xavier Review: "The Cross"
Yankee: "Bird School" and "Purple"

THE
SECRET
VISITOR'S
GUIDE

Bill Stafford

I saw him read one summer in Fairbanks,
the patter between poems itself a poem
because he was like that, fully at home
with words. That lit June night he offered thanks
for some gladness or other, and laid planks
of language that formed a lucky bridge from
one thought to the next. What might seem to some
a plainness too simple for poetry – drank
of poetry when he spoke. I reflected
for years on his writing, could hear him chime,
sly and instructive, as I connected
with my work. The voice said to make time
each morning, to begin early on task,
to learn from failures, to ask and to ask.

PART I

The Cross

Inside's a country
of wolf, bear, coyote,
cat; a river fast and wild
as sin; the field
no one's homesteaded;
a lode of gold
fat as humpback whale.
Tear me. Rip me up.
Inside's half moon,
half island; vast cloud-high
peaks; a dying aspen's last
drop of sap; non-stop blasts
of polar wind; hunger,
the hole where everything goes.

Farming

for Karen

Begin small: a shell of a house
that smells like your grandmother's;
a black dog to shadow you
loading and unloading, splitting
and hauling, raking and sweeping.

Grow potatoes and carrots.
Plenty of garlic and onion.
Spinach, broccoli, zucchini.
Purple, red, and yellow flowers.
Herbs all winter, on the sill.

Your rabbits call you to listen.
Your goats, to remember.
Your horse, to explore further.
Your chickens, to let ghosts run
headless a minute before cleaning.

Coyote Pantoum

I spit this poem
to clear the pain
deep within that comes
from bone. A game

to clear the pain,
yes. A sly yelp
from bone. A game.
Animal help,

yes. A sly yelp.
Coyote in the soul.
Animal help –
this coyote call.

Coyote in the soul,
this body. An ache,
this coyote call
I make. And remake

this body. An ache
like a howl.
I make and remake
myself. My growl

like a howl.
Like coyote.
My self, my growl
of history.

Like coyote,
the pain
of history
changes men.

The pain
deep within comes
and changes men.
I spit this poem.

But For Wilderness

Childless, she claims
her eldest is miles
of alpine ridgetop,
a scramble up a peak
like an arrowhead.

Her next is winter island
of sand, wind, loon,
the sudden blunt need
to strip and run headstrong
into the gray churning.

As friends chatter of theirs
in kindergarten, she braids
fingers over belly, feels
herself swell with jungle,
or tundra, or both.

Noah's Half Sister

A young woman who fell asleep
beneath a blossoming apple tree
woke when a ripe gold one dropped
square on her forehead.
Grumbling – she always grumbled
when suddenly roused from summer's
slumber – she munched
that apple, seeds and all,
and grew amazed. As she ate,
the small orchard filled
with animals. She fed them –
the mouse, a mouthful;
the elephant, a bushel –
and began hiking north.
From aardvark to zebra
the creatures followed
as if in fabulous migration
toward the winter home.

40th Birthday

for Kate Brown

To celebrate she roasted elk, fixed
sautéed morels, wild rice,
and for dessert was treated
to the sky's gift: an orgy
of northern lights. The tingling
within spilled out her eyes
like liquor. Toasting to limitless
intimacy, she refilled the tequila
and slipped outside
to let the moon and stars stare,
to let the last green dancing whip
shoot its spark, to let the brisk
southwest breeze spirit her aloft
into the high desert night.

Rationale

Like a hike, a conversation
can accidentally touch

rare beauty any instant.
"We'll come back,"

one or the other will say,
positive there's no forgetting

this overgrown trail,
that timely opening.

"It's late. Let's keep going."
And so they walk

or talk past that place,
pressing tentatively forward

to what must be.

The Holiness of Shoveling Snow

For half a day the scrape
of metal on gravel, a warm
cold stillness inside the ache
of dig, lift, and fling,
the strain of shaving down
the driveway as if chin

or cheek. Mostly cleared,
you thrust the shovel upright
to lean against, rest,
and see past the truth – birches
snowy as sky, clouds high
and quiet as time, silence

that begs pure light – past
all that white until ghost ravens
flap, phantom salmon leap,
all clamor yes. Regripping
the handle, you dig, lift,
and fling the next simple shovelful.

Gardeners, or Not

Early frost might
    erase our tulips;

Wildfire might
    consume our melons;

Taku gales might
    seize our peas;

Icy rain might
    murder our spinach;

Or coyote might
    abandon us,

making us wanderers
    for life.

Atop Mt. Roberts

for Cliff

When clouds lose themselves
in other clouds, the sky
loses itself in storm.
A conversation takes place
that may or may not include
you, reader, if you were out
hiking, an innocent windless
May morning that turned
unpleasant and cold. Cloudy,
you mutter, summitting
this dark gray peak
that has lost itself
in the mist of wisdom,
accomplishment, and loss.

Anchorage, December 25, 3 P.M.

In sinking afternoon light,
the unattached spirits gather.
Some come as snowflakes,
others as bits of sky, or cloud,
or pieces of dirt hard asleep
under ice. Others as moose,
owl, raven, lynx. It's getting dark –
this winter day so ordinary,
windless, and perfect – when a single
warm breeze from above
blows gentle, strong, miraculous
as a wave. Or a glance. Or a smile.
That's all it takes now
for a whole outer world
to shift ever so slightly –
and for this latest season
to enter, or exit, this earth.

PART II

The Whale Biologist

for Jan and John Straley

Settled in your skiff, warmed
by layers, to find whales
we cut chilled August sea air,
then quickly sped from sunlit
to overcast sky. Talking little

over the motor's roar,
I watched you search, your scan
so intent I almost asked:
Why whales, Jan?
And then I knew: Whales –

the giant keys to our past.
That day, out far, we spotted spouts,
glimpsed telltale flukes. Your glee
was proof: Male and female,
they were at it again.

Orientation

Come, I say. Accompany me
past Conshohocken and Germantown.
Tunnel with me through three hills.
Cross two borders. Settle near a loop.

If you miss a turn, remember steep switch-
backs, the downhill runaway.
If you get lost, remember
the October sun's arc,

and the trail, though tricky,
leads to a room full of books.
On the bed, I've set three thick quilts.
Beside it, a fiddlehead, your favorite plant.

Outside, wind blows leaves off birches.
A raven circles. The first snow
has dusted hilltops. Come, I say.
Accompany me forever.

Alaska Bachelor

Rejected by a Sitka woman,
who flapped like a raven
from love to love, whose
epic discontent in a state
where men were so abundant
led her to grumble that
though the odds were good
the goods were odd. And told
by another missed connection,
a biologist from Fairbanks,
that for a man to snatch
someone wonderful, he'd need
to spot a couple almost
but not quite in trouble,
then do what dirt it took
to pry the two apart,
the bachelor rued that given
his pathological mildness
he'd never mate – until he woke
one morning to the crowbars
that had for so long crossed
his heart. Tossing off the long
sharp pieces of steel,
he felt himself lighten
and lighten. And then he rose.

Big Bed, Big Room

May light streamed in
every window, the housemates
were gone, and he'd begun
kissing his new love – gently,
softly, as deeply as he dared –
when he picked her up,
danced her around that big
upstairs cabin bedroom,
bounced her on the mattress,
lifted her again, tossed her
back down to the sheets,
her yes a sound between squeal
and shriek as he flung myself
to her, felt what must have been
his grizzly rumbling awake.

As that big bed and room
shook with their hunger
and heat, by turns they bit,
burned, groaned, and were opened.

Light Tonight

They can never agree
who saw who first, whether
this summer, this festival,
this tent site, or that.

Only that now, afterwards,
winter, home, a mix of snow,
sleet, freezing rain blowing
offbeat against the windows,

walls, they agree this too
is music as they dreamily turn
toward each other, imagine 2 a.m.
sun with his bright orange fiddle,

moon with her pale little banjo,
eyeing each other a moment
before setting instruments carefully
down in dark hardshell cases.

Fiddle and Banjo

for Scott Marckx and Jeanie Murphy

Two years back,
spotting my friend, Jeanie,
jamming with a guy I knew,
Scott, I paused a moment
to admire the sparkling rabbits
perched pretty as hearts on each
of their shoulders, the critters
then cartwheeling like cheerleaders
before my incredulous eyes.

I wanted to say something,
ask this curious couple
about the animal magic
that had joined the music,
a P.T. Barnum-like fiddle-
banjo trick for the nineties.
But no. Passing silently,
I thought: Don't interrupt –
maybe it's business from above.

The Airport Lounge

You pace. I
sit watching
you pace

faster. Behind
you, the ice-
glazed windows

reveal runways,
gray skies,
the freezing

rain falling
frozen. Honey,
I love you,

but please
sit down.
Our plane

will come
when it comes.
Do you hear?

Bird School

When we cracked the window,
a small crow glided to our bed,
roosted a minute, preened
and squawked, delivered
its raucous lecture.

So we removed all glass,
let in the birds – all sizes,
colors, songs – and studied.
For graduation, we took off
outside, opened wings, flew.

The Larsen / Caulfield / Paul House

To tourists strolling, the Juneau address –
525 W.9th – might seem nothing
extraordinary: a nice-sized, good-looking
house and yard, a solid unpretentious
front, fresh cement on the steps, a new fence.
"Beside Gold Creek and near the Federal Building,"
locals walking past might say, stopping
to study the house they rarely notice.
Wait until they hear experts consider it
the finest Dutch-style two-story Larsen built.
Wait until they see the new interior
with shiny hardwood living room dancefloor.
Wait until friends drop in for contras and squares
with Tom, Jan, Riley, Sal – the house's stars.

Aglow

– for Marianne Jewell

Each morning for how many years now
you slide the windows, point the heart,
then wake to a morning full of doors
you must push open and walk through,
or die. Old doors, splintered doors,
stuck doors, crazy doors – this your path
no matter how broken or glued the lock,
how warped the jamb, how difficult

the knob. Ingenious you, barricaded
time and again, thinking death's
slippery thin fingertips have threaded
the needle at last, you've gathered
faith. An ordinary hour spills
with the delight of grass and wind
fiddling reels, the sea playing piano,
the sun stepdancing across sky

with a leap. Evenings, near sleep,
still patient at the threshold,
you hear everything click into place
with a knock. The doors swing open.
You enter fresh into shininess,
a ten carat ruby polished by light.
Your eyes brighter and brighter.
Iridescence wider and wider.

Difficulty's Last Stand

for Rebecca

Three-quarters up the mountain,
quickly catching myself
as I slipped on switchback,
I could rejoice how my body
had healed: for the first time
in five years I was climbing.
It felt good, I tell you,
putting weight on the knees,
feeling the joints springy,
letting myself disappear
into breath and step.

Then I thought of you,
the you of language,
depth, disease, difficulty,
the you of deliverance
who would want me to make
this hike holy. For you
I ascended past treeline
into the miracle of light.

Fairbanks, 3 A.M.

A night erupting with red dancing,
as if the March dark and cold had mated
to birth electricity, and create
higher color. The meaning of everything,
I thought, a subarctic lightshow living,
freezing, yet boiling to be seen, slated
for now. Lucky me. The red whips skated –
whirling curtains, tapered leaps, slamdancing
pretzels, the ghostly kites a king-size
sky-wide miracle. God's tongue licking it,
I joked to myself. A scarlet tide, maybe.
Or flying vipers. I felt it in my thighs,
the power. Back inside, bed, I bit
my sweet's soft neck. The aurora, baby.

Woman Fisherman

Desolate Togiak, late-May,
herring ripe. My sixth year,
this Bristol Bay fishery

more familiar than ever:
migrating swans and cranes
paddle in ponds,

a 10 p.m. sun paints
the streaked pink sky.
This place floods me,

a tidal wave. I don't know
why my husband left me,
or why I've returned

this spring without him.
It kills me to catch so many
in my nets, alone.

PART III

The Secret Visitor's Guide

I

Fly to Anchorage
and marvel: a shadowy
mountainous business.
Order a taco.

II

Off Goldstream Road,
Fairbanks: solar-
heated cabins, tidy
outhouses out back.

III

Glennallen, Delta, Tok:
at each junction
the spirit of hitchhikers
who've never left.

IV

Downtown Juneau
in October: tourists
gone, legislators absent,
rainy wind, rainy rain.

V

Village life: dream
mud, dust, river,
and frozen ocean
become you. Fly away.

Women's Bay, Kodiak

I descend from clifftop
picking my way through
alders, devil's club,
a weedy marsh, pockets
of shooting stars blooming.
The trail, barely visible,
suddenly winds steeply
to grassy ravine,

shoreline. Low tide.
Wind and sun beating
my face, I step from rock
to rock, almost slip on kelp
before I sit on a boulder,
remove shoes and socks,
letting surf wash over
as some bird calls

to another. The tide
is rising. Shedding clothes,
I walk to where there is
no rock, total sand.
In the shallowness I wade,
plunge, then swim.
The bay water cleanses,
numbs me.

15,000 Feet, Denali

for Jim Lawhon

Blue ice
chips and skitters.

Three breaths. Step.
Right foot. The ax.

His pack
would have him backwards,

tumbling. He trembles,
feels sweat trickle

and clump in his beard.
Above, God's porch,

his summons.
Climb, he hears.

So he kicks.
Foot in. The ax.

Fiddling Jim

If he's not seated in the sunroom
sawing southern G tunes, he's deep
in an armchair, deeper in a book,
or conversing over a cup of tea
about God, women, bachelorhood
in this holy and stubborn world,
or hard at the stove laboring
his soups and breads, or upstairs
hammering, or downstairs drilling,
or catching a glimpse of newsprint
which causes him to wryly dissect
the current Alaskan budget –
our sad fiscal mismanagement,
or . . . *If*. If this is Fiddling Jim,
he's beside a window, all bow arm
and jump fingers, powering through
one more medley of G tunes, then D tunes
for hours upon hours upon hours.

Fiddle Contest, Haines Fair

for Bob Banghart

3 p.m. Saturday, ticket sellers busy
making change despite the weather –
a typical mid-August chill
and mist that fogged the Chilkat Range,
Haines' official drizzle of fall –
more than two hundred people
crammed beneath the tent while others
lingered outside as the fine rain
precipitated a bit harder –
what non-Alaskans term downpour.

The emcee, I stepped to the mike,
scraped a couple of old-time tunes
best I could solo, then called
in turn the nine competitors,
who each performed five-minute sets
accompanied by choice of guitar,
piano, banjo, mandolin, washboard,
one even backed by a clogger
whose stomps delighted the crowd
more than any contestant's bowing.

Afterwards, a judge took me aside:
they'd voted champ the Juneau fiddler
who'd attacked those Cajun numbers
as Dewey Balfa once had. And you,
she grinned, were a perfect lead-off –
anyone out there would have thought
they could jump up and play.

Backstage, I gathered the musicians,
announced the result. The winner
split first prize money ten ways.

Inupiat Country

Geography is a lover
of contour and terrain:
the Alaska tundra,
white hills rising, dune-like,
before silver skies.
Spring, when the winter
freeze breaks up,
ice, rock, wood,
garbage, water
hurtle downriver
to sea.

At 5 a.m.
two kayakers push from port
in splashes
as they tandem paddle past the bend
to fish camp.
One pulls and pulls. The other
pulls
and counts each stroke.
Arrival.
Set nets swell with salmon,
sheefish.

In cool rain
the grandmother takes
three grandchildren.
The high grass prickles.

Picking the nearest hill
clean, always more
blueberries, salmonberries,
early cranberries.
They fill bags,
eating the largest berries
as they do.

One October night
a west wind sweeps
first snow. A thin layer
of ice conceals the strait.
The full moon hides.
Sled dogs yelp
and circle their posts.
Next morning, wind dead,
sun a bright ball,
a shiny white stillness
seduces the land.

Snow Angels

Ten miles into tundra
and hills out of Elim,
hot springs bubble.
Come jump and dip
in the steaming pool
which'll ripple
with our splash.
Sweetheart, to love
is to be afire inside
this frozen earth.
Take me to China –
we'll burn our way.
I want you in the snow.

Eskimo Dancing

One of many who'd married
into Nome, the councilman,
a bald pudgy white guy
who'd kicked around Fairbanks
in the sixties, invited me
to fiddle with the drums,
"take this Eskimo music
into the next century."

Next performance, I sat
beside this smiley politician
who jabbed me twice to say
the old man in the middle
pounding with a stick
was his father-in-law.
I watched the drummers watch
the dancers move: I knew

what looked easy was more
than Inupiat arms and legs
jerking and flailing to banging.
This dance meant the culture.
I might have come forward
and put strings to that sound.
But I was not of that land.

Up the Unalakleet River

If passing through Unalakleet in winter,
borrow snowmachine or dogteam, or ski
the six miles up river ice, and visit
the sometimes hermit who will be pleased
you've stopped for a minute. Proud
of his cabin, let him show you the loft,
the wolf and fox pelts, the box of cigars,
the typewriter and fiddle, the woodstove
and woodpile, the books, the quiet.

Then let this sourdough be (unless
you're a woman, or fellow trapper, musician,
Midwest refugee – then you can linger
for a nip of whiskey, a smoke, maybe hear
how your modest host once strangled
a wolverine, snowshoed out of Stebbins,
emergency flew a plane). Leave an address.
When ready for company, he'll bake a cake,
decorate it himself, invite you to eat.

The Peninsula Blues

Bustling Shishmaref with its tannery
and plans, first time through I fiddled
and guest-starred inside the high school,
third period on, that evening taught
two statewide college writing classes
over phone, later read poetry
for the locals, then played music
past midnight for Joe, the principal,
not quitting until that burly Montanan
pulled out his own crinkly orange
out-of-tune fiddle, rosined the bow,
scratched what he could, a sickening
screech he'd named The Peninsula Blues.
It sounded like a moose kicking a wolf
off a roof, and falling on top of it.

A year later, I returned, walked
the length of that good-natured village
built on a strip of earth that was sinking
into sea. I waved to folks roaring
on snowmachines, bought gum in the store,
passed sunset at the graveyard, watching
one wide pink strip delight a gray half moon.
After my class that night, I visited Joe,
offered to teach him Hell Broke Loose
in Georgia. He laughed, then asked
if I could read a piece I'd shared
the winter before about my Fairbanks pal
who died – could have been set in Philipsburg,
he said. Next morning Bering Air arrived at 9.
I rode a sled to the plane, boarded in the dark.

Stebbins Trip

Sure like the fiddle, he spat, near-toothless
maintenance man who lashed my pack
to the sled, shuttled me to the school
so damaged two years before by fire.
Dropping me off, he waved, smiled,

and was gone, a ghost jockey on machine.
Zero today, flurries, gray still air
like dead skin. A timeless clutter of sixty
or seventy buildings beside a hill, ice,
wilds. Typical, though this hole seemed

extra-disastrous. Seven months after that fire,
two botulism deaths. Since then, several pre-teens
treated for sniffing gasoline. Plus the usual
alcohol casualties. My student here, Sophie,
I knew only from class. A destitute single mother,

she suffered headaches from an ear ailment,
was likely going deaf. Her one-year-old
needed surgery in Anchorage to remove a lump
on his forehead. Her others, three and five,
I guessed were malnourished. I checked

Sophie's journal with a plus. The woman
never complained, accepted hardship with strength –
or was it resignation. I couldn't tell. She read
assignments with a doggedness I imagined inspired
by Bible study, which she'd quit. Intelligent,

she wrote inexplicably bad papers. We'd never met.
I walked into the school, told my business
to the principal, agreed to fiddle in every room
the following morning in exchange for two meals,
a floor to sleep on. Then I was off outside,

laughing at this life I loved – and couldn't wait
to leave. This solo stroll down a lone street.
Poking my head in the local store, I nodded,
a curious customer before shelves
of rotten oranges, apples, onions, moldy cheeses,

cases of Cocoa Puffs, candy bars, dry milk,
knickknacks. I wandered further,
then somehow managed a productive class
despite being locked out of the learning center
(the liaison had lost the key), a power outage

(once Sophie and I climbed in through the window –
this, our introduction – we had a half-hour
bundled in semi-darkness), staticky phone lines
(I had everyone write about frustration),
and the news that Sophie's oldest was sick

(instead of a conference, Sophie would have to
dash home after class; and no, it wasn't a good idea
for me to tag along – I'd risk catching it).
So while the others in Nome, Elim, Wales,
and Shishmaref wrote about frustration,

Sophie and I chatted about our lives,
our wonderful meeting, our plans. I shared
what I could that next half-hour about reading,

writing, books, attending college. Ken, Sophie said,
her right hand on my forearm. You're a good teacher.

I know you're doing your best and I'm not so good.
I'll study harder. I want to learn.
You are learning, Sophie, I said. Yes, Ken, I know,
she said, and then asked why my eyes were so full
of tears. Next morning, the bilingual teacher

led me around, told each primary grade about a fiddler
named Byrd she never forgotten who roamed here
fifty years back. Now listen good, she ordered the kids.
Friendly place, Stebbins. Farthest north Yup'ik village.
Shtebbins, they called it. Their English a natural lisp.

The Icelanders Come to Nome

Ugly site,
the architect noted, deplaning.

Must you smoke?
the bookkeeper asked their cabby.

Why all this trash?
the professor questioned, pointing.

This is not the arctic –
this is a disgrace,
muttered the psychologist.

Catching Nome's face,
heart, spirit.
Missing the joints.

Christmas Party, Anvil Mountain
Correctional Center

For the third straight year a gym
full of tables, a lunch spread
from reindeer to fry bread to jello,
the usual inmates serving, the rest
queuing behind paid civil servants
and volunteer guests. I filled

my plate with meats, chose a chair
away from others, began to eat,
curious how the seats beside me
would play. To my right,
Bennett Ooyapuk soon sat, joked
his research paper on whaling –

an incomplete from two springs back –
would be finished "maybe next week."
To my left, Ricky Tom, from Stebbins,
knocked over a sticky purple drink
as he settled to his seat, and muttered
something about an aunt dying.

I rose, one of the first for seconds,
loaded up this time with salad,
rice, a bowl of moose stew. Someone,
meanwhile, was standing at my place,
a white looking like he'd wandered in
by mistake, like neither prisoner

nor Samaritan. Eyeing me fully,
he met my stare, didn't budge
until I cleared my throat, scanned
the big hall, prepared to leave.
Then, taking my tray, he grunted,
"Not so fast, teacher. You're with me."

Breakers Bar

Slipping in, he grabbed the stool to my left,
loudly ordered a Bud as I took the hand
he offered. Smiling as we shook, he squeezed
my fingers harder, didn't let go, tightening
to deeper bone. He whispered: *Mr. Bigshot*
with a computer, you think just because you left here
and wrote poems, you know this place
and my people, don't you. Think you know me,
don't you.
          I regarded him
as evenly as I could, and when I wiggled my hand
to get loose, he suddenly upped the pressure.
I imagined tendon ripping, a pain
both foreign and familiar. *I could break your hand,*
and I will if you don't ask the barmaid
for her phone number. I want her number,
he hissed, nodding her way. Grinning,
she approached, holding a can and a glass.
You <u>know</u> what I want, he grumbled, and gripped me
harder, one more notch, and I thought of his wife then,
a white woman I once briefly worked with,
the marriage always subject to rumor.
<u>Ask</u> her, he muttered as the barmaid served the beer.
Sorry, was all I could say, and he laughed then,
let my hand go, and slapped my back.
The woman stood there a minute as we talked
about the slow night, the new building going up
on Front Street, the weather, as the Eskimo
downed the beer, ordered two vodka shots.
You missed your chance, white man, he chortled

as she turned her back to pour. I watched her
set two small glasses of clear liquid on the counter
in front of us, then watched him gulp.
You don't know nothing! he shouted,
seeing me head for the door, my liquor untouched.

Beyond Knifepoint

for J.N.

Say that God operates as a drunk bully surgeon
with a grudge, who sits you without anesthesia
in his shiny chair as he goes to work.
"God," you sputter, teeth grinding, the hours
passing as minutes, or weeks. It hurts worse
than losing a lover, or a child. Worse
than a parent's death, this cutting open
to soul, this taking a golden edge
of wing, this stitching back up.

Afterwards, alone in your dustless room,
the days suffer by. Sun, his scalpel. Moon,
his taunt. Every little thing
of this world like a blade of pain. God
laughing at you in his God way, bragging
that he owns you. Sleep punctures.
The pillow draws blood. Never have you felt
so tired, or awake. Doctor God. Write him
this prescription. Let him practice on himself.

The Boscos of Newtok

The popular boy fell in the river
that September evening, never splashed back.
Twelve years old. The whole village felt an ache –
the ache the world has suffered forever.
Grieving men, their grieving wives, remembered
the boy in their prayers. His absence they'd take
home to their rooms, hold tight. Then a small crack
in the loss as men and women shivered,
gasped. Bosco was the name of the boy who drowned.
Bosco. Next summer the village added
Bosco Thomas, Bosco John, Bosco James,
Bosco Charles. Newtok had become the ground
for Boscos. Bosco George too. And Bosco Fred.
Boys who'd become men – the Boscos of dreams.

Pilgrim Hot Springs

Past Noralee's, past Banner Creek,
the Nome River snaky and slithery
and low in brush, past Salmon Lake
on up the Taylor Highway, gravel
and dust that cut dry hilly tundra
with a pebbly swath of grit, until
fifty miles down the dead-end road
a fork, and he cut left, saluted

the first brave stands of trees
out of Nome. Another few miles
he shut off the motor in the lot
of the old missionary school, swigged
from his water bottle, took in
the smells, the leaves, the orange
and red wildflowers with names
he didn't know. Mid-evening, the sky

deep blue but for the wispy clouds
disintegrating like forlorn ghosts,
he strolled toward the tubs. A man
and woman splashed in the big one,
caused him pangs: he'd been so long
between lovers. None in Nome,
the dear friends who'd helped him
survive the recent disaster

couldn't be with him now. Glad
the small tub was empty, he climbed
onto its planked deck, hung his clothes
on a nail, eased himself into the hot
bubbly pool. Through the chicken wire,
a first pink of dusk. He felt lonely
and sad then. So natural before soaking
into the company and light of tomorrow.

Honorary Alaskans

for Sedge Thomson, and maybe you

Inquisitive, you ponder maps,
pronounce simpler place names – Kake,
Wrangell, Sitka, Tok, Nome,
Barrow, Homer – then the twistier –
Yakutat, Unalakleet, Tuntululiak,
Kotzebue, Kwigillingok, Iliamna.

Inquisitive, you take journeys
which might include a night's sleep
on the deck of the Taku or Malaspina,
a misty hike up Mt. Ripinski, a paddle
into a shining Kachemak Bay cove, a sunlit
1 a.m. stroll the length of downtown Ester.

Inquisitive, you'll hear a local
refer to Ketchikan as Tijuana, Alaska;
you'll learn Anchorage is *Los* Anchorage
(a mere half hour from what's truly Alaska);
you'll imagine you'd not just survive winter
in Talkeetna or Haines – you'd thrive.

Inquisitive, you return north a minute
or two daily, plan next year's trip,
then the one after, and take leave
a moment – even if it's over there
in an office, or right here onstage –
and then take leave a moment more.

PART IV

Toward Clarity

Slow and subtle as months
dissolving, as shrouds rustling,
the brain's own brain knows
what has been done, and how
to undo it. First, by listening

to the muse's restless pecking,
the inner brain mishears *plane wreck*
as *change next*, so salves
bruises with poems. The body
heals in half-steps and bumbles.

And the brain of the brain's
own brain? That deeper layer
pulls its shades, and sees pink
to the east. Yes, on time
for what appears like today.

Plane Crash Story, Continued

Everyone wanted to know,
so I told them, I thought,
until two weeks later
when I'd hashed the accident
yet again. When that listener
shrugged and said everyone
he'd talked to knew the story
better than I, how I didn't
even know my plane had skipped
on hitting the hillside, had touched
luckily not once, but twice,
had skipped on snow like a flung stone,
at last landing just short
of a thousand-foot drop-off,
I just looked at him, amazed.
And this too became part
of my story: knocked out
by that first gigantic smash,
I had to rely on others
to tell me the facts.

Grant Aviation, Piper Saratoga

A long Nome sunset slowly reddening
the west, iced hills like sugar
or vanilla, we detoured by Olson Air
to see whether the plane I'd crashed in
had, as rumored, been towed there. Yes,
and it stood as gargantuan artifact
ten feet from the road, propeller demolished,
wings and frame bent, dented, thrashed.
"I don't think I know what I'm looking at,"
I told my pal, who answered, "Aiee, Aiee, Aiee.
Worse than I thought. You don't want to know."
Then said the damage meant I'd hit hard,
been spared by something greater than luck.
"And to think your last sight on earth
might have been this," he pointed inside
the windshield to a Mickey Mouse doll
dressed as a sorcerer's apprentice.
"Aiee, Aiee, Aiee." He shook his head.
We looked a minute more, clambered back
in the truck, then backed up, turned around,
headed to the big Alaska terminal
where I was to board the night jet out.

Forehead Scars

People regarded me
as they might a Rorschach.
"The mark of Cain," I heard
one friend say. "Eye magnet,"
pronounced another. "Badge
of the North," remarked a third.
"A Y, or V, or a dyslexic F.
Or maybe a Sanskrit character
that means: Fell out of sky
and hit something hard."
                                        "A tulip
a neat little kid might draw."
"A question mark." "A red crescent."
"Zipperhead." "A European seven,"
"Not too bad." "Really, really bad."
"Are you going to sue?" "Who died?"
Looking in the mirror, I saw my own:
"Fish hook. Skin dent. Crime.
The survivor's brand. Crash cult
love tattoo. A mystery. A reminder.
Spring. One hundred stitches.
Tissue healing, the lines to fade."

The Inner Wreck

Nearing four weeks after,
I woke one night, body tensed
as if late or lost, woke
the next, forehead bandaged,
spirit drained from a car wreck
nightmare, the broken glass
raining fine shiny slivers.
What then? Back to those
three hours between crash
and rescue, the airplane
on jagged tundra hill, where
a psychologist might say
trauma was imprinted
for keeps. Or further back,
childhood, where my bone
took in the nowhere drive
and smash that was family.
Say my brother suffers
massive head wounds, and dies
in tomorrow night's dream.
What does this say for me?
To live is to experience,
accept, peel back the layers.

Minor Head Injury

Not brain damage, not quite, but a feeling
of damage. Not soft in the head, not quite,
but a hard knowing of the head's unquiet,
the brain in a slow, most subtle healing
that, though full, will take time, cells resettling.
Each long sunny afternoon saddens. Night
is better, in bed early, reading light
bright. I wake later, stare at the ceiling,
then go to bed properly. It's okay,
I realize, to live this. Humanity
welcomes its own shadowy borderline,
a worm wriggling, earth an ashen-gray.
Holding tightly, I cradle sanity,
solaced that this life, though topsy, is mine.

Plane Crash Stories

I didn't hear them all, not all,
but I heard the one about the plane
that took down the lone tree
between Dillingham and Togiak,
the single landmark worth a damn
in that wilderness. And I heard
the one about the bold stunt pilot
who came within feet of recovering
from a crowd-pleasing spin. And the one
about the flight that was missed
because of a freakish change
in itinerary. And the one
where the top pilot's instruments
went haywire. And the one
with the dentists who died
near where I went down,
same conditions and season.
And when I left Nome, returned
to Juneau, I heard even more,
including some I'd heard up north,
this fact altered, that added.

The Further Work

Think of the brain
as the cellular door,
then think of it
after it's been whacked
worse than any warp.
Like the usual home
handyman task, the repair
takes twice the time
you'd like, or longer,
because doors demand
the further work.
Worry if you must
though worry won't ease
the wait. The brain
fixes the brain best
through nightshirt leaps
of measurement and dream,
a dark routine offset
by occasional daytrips
to the hardware place
where the soul hangs.
You don't do a thing
but stay out of the way
and listen for the brain
to say: Perfectly fine,
you can walk back in –
look around and see
what I've added
to the living room,
kitchen, bedroom, bath.

One More Effect of Fog

Because I survived a plane wreck, I can joke
how one friend named it "a good career move,"
how another deadpanned, "You'll make a fortune
teaching people how to make sixty grand
by crashing and suing." Truly, my accident
was no more heroic than any sudden bike, auto,
motorcycle mishap, no more traumatic
than ordinary heart surgery, back surgery,
cancer, divorce, nothing more than another
long twisty story of collision, crumple,
bloodletting, loss, a lucky story
that led to slow healing and release.
One more scar to point to and forget,
save for nights alone before you,
whoever you are. You.

March 2nd, Again

I flew East from Seattle
(first surviving the long city
airport bus ride
where a man my age, curious
about my big pack, asked
if I wasn't perhaps sleeping
in the bushes somewhere),
dozing in my window seat
for the length of Wyoming,
this the exact hour
and day I'd once flown
the coast from Brevig to Nome.
Waking from the nap, having knocked
my head against plastic,
momentarily displaced,
I recalled that former flight –
that sudden hit, that far
greater jolt, the blood
all over my face – then reopened
my book. In plane wreck years,
I'd just turned two.

PART V

September 11, 2001

Austin

This is no poem
about planes hijacked and flown
into New York City buildings,
cameras catching the surreal, endless
snippets – some edited, some not –
of towers on fire awhile,
then suddenly collapsing, the heap
a mix of concrete, dark
smoke, bodies, ash, everywhere
the rubble – and that ignores
a third plane hijacked and flown
into the Pentagon, a fourth
plowing into a Pennsylvania field,
the thousands dead. That's the poem
television writes. Underneath is another –
strange world of good and evil,
love and hate, great anger
and even greater faith.
Nothing ever changes. Everything has.
We'll need friends, family, music.
A language that transcends.

October 11, 2001

The bombing of Afghanistan –
the thick newspaper coverage
continues. Column by column,
section by section, the obvious
response to this impossible fall.
Safety. Retaliation. Security.
Counterattack. Anthrax. Rubble.
Headlines buzz horror. Though
the odd letter to the editor suggests
we're not at war with terrorism,
or the Taliban, but with shadows,
or mosquitoes. Or ourselves.
Yes, a dark season that will end
when we stop the fighting. If we can.

November 11, 2001

God Bless $23 America,
budget motels in Flagstaff,
Fresno, and Eureka proclaim,
their sloppily designed sign-making
sounding like a wry Allen Ginsberg.
God Bless $23 America.
The flags out two months now
at car dealerships, hair salons,
haberdasheries, taco stands.
God Bless $23 America,
$46 America, $52 America,
$79 America, $118 America.
God Bless Our President Bush
who tells us to keep shopping.

Earlier today I sailed to Canada.
Immigrations, Vancouver Island,
I was led to an interrogation room,
was asked the same questions
the inspector at the desk had.
Once more I offered
my driver's license, my ferry ticket back,
my next week's plane ticket to Anchorage,
explained I was an artist, answered
that beyond Anchorage I was going
to Virginia, then to New Mexico,
and, yes, was here in Victoria
to visit a friend, and, no,

had never worked in Canada.
Hours later I read how a Canadian
had her journal searched
at the border, was permitted entry
only after having customs bully her
about what she wrote, return her
passport and car keys in a garbage can.
Over the phone that evening, I heard
a friend tell a story about an eavesdropping
off-duty F.B.I. man leaving a café,
but not before boasting to people a table away
that in a month he'll be able
to arrest them for what they just said.
Occasionally I've watched the news
the past week from one of my $23 motel rooms.
God Bless America. More bombs,
the odd mistargeted strikes.

December 11, 2001

Anchorage

for Pat, Robin, Andrea

Three months ago they died,
the conspicuous and inconspicuous,
the double-quick and super-slow,
the ones in silk, in paisley,
in cotton. Three weeks ago
you told me how you've felt off
ever since, as if Mercury
and Pluto had been exchanged,
every star, too, gone wrong
so that even constellations
were now unrecognizable. The night,
you said, was an industrial park.
And the day, with its spoilage,
a dump. Three days ago I drove
from Fairbanks to Anchorage,
from minus thirty to zero, left the radio
alone those three hundred plus miles,
played two CDs of old-time fiddle music.
Easy to imagine droning strings
powered the truck past the Nenana gray,
the Healy dusk, the wilderness evening.
Easy to imagine the world was
as it's always been – deep, dark,
remarkable. Three hours ago
we were on the phone. Have you
changed, you asked. I sat thinking
how everyone I know is hectic

and broke – just as before.
Only now our government
demands to know those exact
numbers – and thoughts – too.

January 11, 2002

Needles

Between San Francisco and Flagstaff
I buy the Las Vegas daily, take in
its bold headline: high level nuclear
waste dump set for Yucca Mountain,
seventy miles northwest. Further down,
far right column, a smaller story
about the collapse of Enron, new links
to the president's office. The seven
U.S. deaths from a helicopter accident
in Afghanistan fall midway between.
Getting back to normal, I think,
and ponder energy, the Arab world,
the "normal" we've come to expect.

February 11, 2002

Chapel Hill

. . . Tuesday, February 12, and I recall
nothing on yesterday's front page
about terrorism, only further Enron rumblings,
a Salt Lake Olympic feature,
though today we're on "highest alert."
More Saudis, apparently, according
to sources, are roaming this country . . .

. . . and because I sit in a café
eating lunch, reading the paper,
occasionally glancing to watch the news
scroll across TV screen,
I'm doubly alerted. Everything's at risk . . .

. . . though this isn't the first time
I've wondered why, in this terror-driven
time, hasn't the enemy blown up
the odd bridge in rural Kansas
or Wisconsin, bombed a deserted
Utah or Montana strip mall, created
real havoc in out-of-the-way places
that would have vibrated
the Trade Center horror . . .

. . . why not indeed, I wonder,
as I leave all four sections
on the counter, pay my bill,
walk out to take my chances . . .

March 11, 2002

New Orleans

Where the streets have names
like Arts, Pleasure, Music,
Mystery, I've lived
the past fortnight
in a clean-enough
motel room five miles
from the Quarter.
The *Do Not Disturb* sign
hanging on my outside knob
reflects my days. Nights
I cruise past those streets
with the names I like
on my way to the dance halls.
Terpsichore. Calliope. Royal.
Rampart. Toulouse. As long
as I don't think about world affairs
or money, I'm happy.

April 11, 2002

Minneapolis

Last night I drove from Milwaukee,
napping once in a church parking lot
past Baraboo, again in a travel stop
near Menomonie. The past two weeks:
Galesburg, Chicago, Ann Arbor, Detroit,
Cleveland, Buffalo. Palestinian suicide
bombers terrorize that region. Afghanistan
remains incomprehensible, as does our
national government. This morning I'll appear
on Minneapolis community radio, the weekly
literary show where I'll fiddle and talk, read
a few poems. This afternoon, rehearsal. Evening,
the performance. *Don't quit your day job,*
I say to everybody who claims
my life romantic. And point to erratic
schedule and pay, occasional audience,
the lack of a love life. It's the latter
that's the killer, I think, as I walk
a half-dozen blocks in the rain, grateful
today I have the freedom and resources
to complain only of this.

May 11, 2002

Minneapolis

This shouldn't be, I think, this loop
that finds me back in Minneapolis: more
spring rain, my days still erratic, occasional,
and without significant love. Last week,
Manhattan, I met someone at a party
in Midtown. We subwayed back
to the East Village, drank tea past midnight
at a sidewalk table, shared dessert,
arm-in-arm strolled to her building
as we planned our meetings the next days.
Parting, we kissed twice,
then I leaned in for another, feeling understood
at last. The next evening I performed
in Tribeca, blocks from ground zero,
a place I didn't want to go just to gawk,
so didn't go at all. I had no time
was my excuse, preferring to attend BookExpo,
the huge national book industry convention,
as a "non-industry visitor." (Apparently,
my two volumes for a respected
New Mexico publisher plus a local gig
big enough to get listed in *The New Yorker*
didn't count in the book business.) At the club,
my new friend never showed. The next day,
unable to contact her, I left messages,
and ended my time in the city two days later
without hearing back. Just as well, probably,
though I didn't know why. On a scale of one
to ten, the city is back to eight, an old friend,

who's made his life in Manhattan, told me
my last night in town. I'd nodded, my mind
on the woman who disappeared, and the upcoming
five thousand miles from New York City
to Anchorage. The country, too, I might have said
is eight. And me, here tonight, back again
in Minneapolis, I'm single and irritable.

June 11, 2002

Anchorage

Lots of very pregnant American
women, I read somewhere. No surprise,
really, the past September slowdown, eyes
searching eyes, the world atilt, time to question
this choice and that, and to fall back in
love with a beloved – or be unwise
with a stranger. Was it the sheer size
of the towers? TV screens again and again
replaying smoke and fire? What else to do
but seek relief. And leave it to our father
in D.C. to reassure that nothing
could have been done. Though now we're coming to
uncover one Bush untruth after another.
So we're the ones to do the answering.

July 11, 2002

Another 12-hour day on the road,
I play the same solo old-time
fiddle tapes I always play, puzzle
today's versions of the same
events I always puzzle. Why
hadn't the border patrol
at Prince Rupert asked
about the boxes in back
of my minivan? (Especially
when I was prepared
this time to expect the worst.)
When would I catch
that big break with my work?
(So what that my finances
had recently progressed
from ruinous to tenuous –
I was still in debt.)
What had happened
to the young woman whose face
was on posters everywhere?
(She'd gone missing hitchhiking
en route to a festival in Smithers.)
Why hadn't the September 11th
terrorists followed with small-scale
destruction? (Why haven't we suffered
on our soil the same unstoppable attacks
that occur near-daily in the Mideast?)

At Prince George, as a big sun
lords over dry bright skies,
I take a right, today's one turn.
All afternoon into early evening,
asking myself more of the same,
I continue rolling south. Hope,
even the twilight shines.

August 11, 2002

Elkins, WV

Many canaries, many mineshafts,
a line I scribbled on a paper scrap
months ago, and set on the dashboard
to be buried beneath the occasional
important receipt, the odd map, the other sheets
I didn't want to lose. *Many canaries,*
many mineshafts, and I may have
written those words sailing interstate 90
west through North Dakota, or 84
southeast between Boise and Salt Lake,
though what does it matter, really,
another cross-country trip, four words
insistent as litter, louder than radio.
Many canaries, many mineshafts,
and ironic how it's in West Virginia
on this hot sunny Sunday I've rediscovered
the phrase, looking for something else.
Only an hour ago we sat in the parlor
and I listened to a discussion
of which nearby caves would be safest
in case of disaster – and I learned how
our most powerful national officials
had already planned for such contingency
and had secured the largest, so could
run this country indefinitely
from some remote underground compound.
And was reminded why I'd bothered writing.
Canaries, mineshafts, bin Laden, Bush.

September 11, 2002

New Orleans

Newspaper stories have run
a week now. Editors agree
no one knows whether to make
the day regular or holy
even as the front page turns
sensational – the memory is bigger
than our Iraqi plans. Yesterday I heard
a local broadcaster mistake
celebrate for *commemorate*
as he announced today's activities.
I'm back in New Orleans, yes,
commemorating the day as I do
so many others, by phone calling
and emailing, by visiting schools
to meet with teachers and administrators.
You'd think I'd be tired of this
hustle peddling poetry and music
to people who are mostly indifferent –
and you'd be wrong. I've lived
in Alaska seventeen years, and loved
the gorgeous light, the distant villages,
the kinds of folks you find up north.
I've loved that life as I love this one
I'm living now – the other morning biking
Bourbon Street at 10 a.m., humidity
a two-hundred-pound ghost weight,
for once on my way nowhere
in particular – the coming weeks due
in Charleston, Denver, Durango,

Flagstaff, jobs I've contracted
through the oddest mix of magic
and grants. The man who wrote
the poem about a wheelbarrow
and the chickens used to say
what many hunger to know
are in poems – though difficult
to find. If he's right, and a few
are sated here, I'm blessed.

Where There's War

Austin, January 20, 2003

Where there's war, there's an anti-war
of writers writing, readers reading,
veterans recalling what they served for –

to make the world more
open for children, to share understanding.
Where there's war, there's an anti-war,

and in between a heavy warped door
old, creaky, and infuriating. Seething
veterans, recalling what they served for,

can't find sense in making only the poor
pay for the needs of the rich – and suffer dying.
Where there's war, there's an anti-war

of you and I walking into the music shop, the food store,
greeting friends, finding peace in being.
We're veterans who recall what we serve for –

not god, not country, but the chore
after chore that is the daily chore of living.
Where there's war, there's an anti-war –
writers, readers, veterans recalling what we serve for.

Sestina for George W. Bush

From the beginning I've wondered why
no one has named your war
Vietraq. I've heard it called a lie,
an outrage, a quagmire. But where's
the context? Face it, W,
you're going down in history

as the American Hitler. History
loves extremes. And we know why.
Big winners and losers make it new. And you, you,
you gave us not just war,
but failure of failures — where
instead of letting a sleeping dog lie,

you threw a pail of lye
on the beast. You're making history,
W, the strange kind, where
you've reinvented x and y
to equal suffering and war.
And z, z now looks like W.

Yes, you've rewritten language, W.
Orwell's fashionable. No, it's not a lie
when it comes from up top. Sure, war
is really peace, Truths are false. History
becomes future. Why turns into why
not. On and on no matter where

we look. So, W, where
next? To Syria, W?
Iran? North Korea? Why?
Why not? It's all the same lie
in your hands--the history
of a meaningless, useless war

that will lead to deeper war
not just in Iraq, but everywhere.
Don't you believe in History,
W? I know you believe in God, W,
a most undemocratic god that, no lie,
favors you, Texas, and America. Why

not look at other wars, W.
You'll find, yes, your God lies.
Study the Nazis; study Vietnam. History shows why.

Sonnet for George W. Bush

You're proof anyone can be president –
that is if you're born to a family
of million-dollar houses: Miami,
New York, Houston. It helps, too, if you went
to Yale (connections, yes), missed getting sent
to Vietnam (yes, connections). You see
our freedom-lovers prefer pedigree
to talent. No, we don't honor talent
unless it's a talent for bankrupting
small business, confusing drugs, corrupting
age-old security. How I too might
have become president: Simply delight
in the climb up one back, another, one more,
bankrolling corporations, fucking the poor.

PART VI

Purple

Pretend you're a cat
on your eighth life:
the sky, the clouds,
the trees – the world's
a bruise as you leap
clawing ledge to ledge.
One fabulous death left
to fritter, your purr
knows gravel, your meow
a memory of strawberry.
For the first time
you find yourself musing
about muskrat, rabbit,
the meaning of mouse.
Lucid, vulnerable, shy,
you edge to your ninth.

At the Intersection of Market and Vine

Love is timeless, the country-
western singer drawled, car radio crackling.
I turned the knob, the light changed
green, and I lurched
to the next intersection,
the next red light
where I heard on the radio
a poet's running for president.

I didn't believe it,
not for a second, but I listened
close, ear stapled to the dashboard speaker,
waiting for an interview which I guessed
might be conducted in iambic pentameter,
or better, spoken in long muscular lines laced with play,
ending in an image –
a field of delphinium,
or something equally poetic, blue.

Maybe a poet *was* running for president,
but as I listened in that steamy rush-hour,
and hoped for a morsel
of super-visionary truth, I heard
a sophisticated melody
followed by a repetition of this:

Snakes in the air
Cows in the sea
Burger King French Fries
One, Two, Three

The commercial lasted exactly one half minute –
I timed it – and when the light changed,
my fist felt like a loudspeaker
so I pressed hard on the horn
until the car in front of me accelerated,
the goddamned coyote.

Instrument Auction

for Col. Sandy Bradley

All preview day, folks peruse mandolins,
accordions, ukuleles, banjos, bugles –
pickety-plunk meets ratcheting cacophony
for a shot, a beer, and a smoke
in a five thousand square foot elevator
going nowhere. How many dozen out-of-tune
samplers practicing for a parade? Random
orchestral warm-up cut and pasted to make
no-category music. Everywhere in the shifting
abyss, snatches of avante garde symphonies
disappearing in holes. Sick porcupines
chased by hounds. Though somewhere in that din,
a curious player takes a sun-blistered fiddle
out of ripped case, tightens a bow,
runs the horsehair across all four strings,
fixes on something squirrely, quietly in C,
tricky little runs edging up, up, up,
then quickly shooting down a tree.

The Violinmakers

A few pieces of wood, some tools, a shop,
and the violinmakers are in business.
Mapped, curved, shapely maple carvings. Stretched fists.
Female torsos. Chiseled fellows. Odd teardrop
bleeding into odd teardrop. Tabletop
for fat ladybug or ant. Metaphors miss
like each finished instrument misses
and misses. Past craft, it's building a prop
between duty and luck, improbable
by-product of hours obsessing this
or that glue, stain, or cut. A sly, subtle
art, violinmakers run businesses
that create and sell handsome strung boxes
from near nothing. Musical carpenter foxes.

Fiddlesticks

for Wilson Douglas, and for George Sleichter

Except for the odd rag in E, B-flat,
or F, or some super-eccentric rhythm,
run, or note – most old-time fiddle tunes
sound the same. Though I once heard
an elderly mountaineer, his voice
a whispery rasp from throat cancer,
say you could tell everything
about the man by the way he played.
That West Virginian then raised fiddle
to chin, pushed bow across strings,
as simple as that gave the music lift,
and there I was in the midst
of a crookedy joy – almost circular,
almost square – that made great pain
shoot straight to nothing.

The Caller

A contra or square dance without caller?
Couples mill the floor, overfill the odd set
or wavy line as band members suggest
mutiny, until some brave soul hollers
for the man to bow to his own, swing her
once and go on to the next, don't forget
a great big old bow to the one now met,
swing her high, swing her low, and allow her,
gent, to go back to her own, you the same
as you balance that original dame,
swing her quick and promenade her home, home,
promenade her home, then you leave your own,
go on to the next. So back to place, all.
(Callers stir the music that stirs the hall.)

Music Party

for Sandy Bradley, and Jere and Greg Canote

This one's got drunk howling mariachis perched
on rainy porchsteps, an insistent cat screeching
operatic harmony, wanting in. Front hall,
the swing session: an elfin redhead in pink
neon socks croons a sassy-sweet Tea For Two
above jazzy mando riffs, violin cutting in
like a jive car horn, her own tiptoe-y bass.
One bedroom's Round Peak string-band standards;
another's Cajun accordion; in the kitchen corner
beside a table loaded with leftover potluck
pasta salad, apple pie, beans, rice, chips, ham,
melted ice cream, empty bottles, turkey carcass
picked clean, the saucy blonde dance-calling
host fixes a perfect red rose in her hair,
snags a partner to clog to slippery twin
fiddle, banjo, guitar – the stomping wonders'
bucks and chugs to break down Saturday night
until dawn, C tune by ragged C tune back-up.

The Galax Sound

for Bev, June, Rose, Tara

From Galax take highway 221,
the hills rising and falling
crooked, as if spooked. If you love
those mountains' screechy ghosts,
stop the car, remove the roof,
then shoot northeast all day

aiming for Philadelphia like a hawk.
That's the way to die: night
falling, moon rising, driving
the convertible hard into dusk.
A dark engine drones the fiddle
that makes the heart beat faster.

Irish Tea

In the juggle of job, geography,
child-rearing, art, sometimes the only
quiet is at the kitchen table,
a pot of tea, perhaps a bowl of custard,
a visitor. The conversation – a fine
visible thread one or the other
occasionally pulls tight – stretches
from Ireland to Alaska, culture
to creature, mad experience
to dizzy present. How to best sew
the dream? The question follows
the line we daily stitch:
the journey inside. On the stove
water steams. Another pot suffices.

Laura Louise

She asks mom for permission
to kiss the moon, lick a flower,
to click on her dad's new computer.
A precocious eight, unself-conscious
as light, this quiet slip of a kid
slides from blind mice to Mozart
in a single whiny fall of piano.
Perfect as an egg, she'll trample off
mornings to school, lunchbox banging.
Laura Louise, troublesome as any muse,
honey-colored hair like some trick
marriage of shampoo and sun.
She goes to bed clutching a camera
after praying to god for a green zebra.

Vertigo in New Mexico

Talk about an attack. Two days in Santa Fe
wrung me like two hundred. The city different:
accident-happy mestizo taxi drivers
tailgating on ice, The All-Critter Café
where the "new" menu boasts coyote chili
and birdbrain pudding, a near weapons center
that booms civic economy. One exception:
Friday, southbound in I-25 freeway traffic,
listening to a folk show on public radio,
I saw a deep auburn sunset suddenly
turn pink, a lone cirrocumulus
silhouette dead southwest in slow dissolve.
Just then an a cappella gospel number –
I Saw the Light – hit the air.
From the first bar a stupendously rare
exuberance, as if Reverend Gary Davis himself
had joined gospel greats The Five Trumpets,
and the sextet sung so hard god melted
the sky. I jumped in, basso profundo,
also banging the dashboard top with a fist.
Too bad some asshole in a cowboy hat driving
a Mercedes – probably a weapons center exec –
shot me a finger as I slid into "heaven
coming down," the last words, last refrain.
Still singing, stretching that last syllable's
note, going as low as my lungs would go,
I unrolled the window, shot a finger back.

But the fucker was gone, lost in the red
lit dusk. So long Santa Fe! Goodbye
desert! Hallelujah! Sing it, Reverend!
Sing it, brothers and sisters! *I saw the light!*
I saw the light from the heaven coming down!

High Tide

At twilight the mountain,
cloud, and sky go violet,
the cove dull silver,
and with sidearm flicks
a boy skips a pink stone
over the surface.

Four splashes: mountain
and cloud bump, the purple
sky dies, a westerly
kicks in, and raindrops
big as pearls
wash the child away.

The Snackers of This Earth

God is nibbling
the world: a famine
here, a monsoon there,
an appetite for the odd
volcano, avalanche,
or quake. God's
dutiful children, sweet
men and women, fix
their own: dammed
rivers, shaved mountains,
salmon, wolf, beaver,
owl. Coyote for kicks.

Dawn Coyote

Dreamt she caught
    the moon
and lost.

        Dreamt she mislaid
    her navel
        and searched.

Dreamt she bought
    a red boat
          that sailed
      bruised seas
       in a whoosh.

Dreamt she cried
    trying to swim
  back across.

        Dreamt she found herself
drowning,
      sucked
   like a stone
    down
      a long
        inky chute.

Dreamt she slept

a year,

woke splashing,

kicking,

stabbed

by light.

Dreamt water

broke

spilling dolphin,

sunfish, millions

of pearls.

Juneau Vets

Some third floor corner of the Alaskan Hotel,
amidst banjo, banjo-uke, bass, vintage Gibson,
a half dozen fiddlers paused between tunes
to pass more beers, jokes, a near-empty bottle,
then somehow commenced counting the almost deaths
to mountain, river, road, weather, these musician-
survivors of broken luck that cracked just right,
so tonight could boast of ninety-foot falls,
colliding trucks, iced planes and fog-shrouded hills,
the improbable mistakes that ended in rescue,
hospital, bandage, cast. Every single player
just a matter-of-fact Alaskan who now remembered
both a certain banjoist and brother fiddler
lost from the room, two missing friends whose last
tune would always be their maybe-accidental fate.
Someone raised a beer in toast, another kicked
a breakdown in D, and the group swiftly flew down
old fingerboards to set off an avalanche, and race.

On Propaganda

"Harvesting trees," a euphemism
for clear-cutting old-growth spruce. A joke,
I thought, the first time I heard the phrase. Look,
harvest doesn't mean to gather once in
several hundred years. Harvest means season
upon season, plum or bean, steady work
in orchard or garden, fresh food to cook
and eat, an annual celebration.
Listen. For "pre-emptive strike" hear *invasion*.
For "Liberate Iraq," hear *supply U.S. oil.*
For "Saddam" or "Bin-Laden," hear *scapegoat.*
To object, there's no single solution.
One response: contemplate wind, sky, soil;
plant seeds; wait. When words get defiled, take note.

John Haines, Fairbanks, June 2004

I recognized him at once, old poet
aided by cane. He made a steady path
across the student union floor. The flash
of years made me his shadow, or son. He wrote
of the Interior, of flood and drought,
distinctive, hard-eyed lines. On his long watch
this river valley had changed. The death
of the country, some would argue, and note
homes now dotting deep woods, so much land tamed.
The old poet turned, then stood before
the automatic teller, punched several keys.
Out popped the bills. I lay back, studied him
as I would caribou, wolverine, bear.
Finding paper, pen, I didn't dare breathe.

About the Author

A twenty-year resident of Alaska, Ken Waldman has made his living the past decade touring North America as "Alaska's Fiddling Poet." He has published poems and stories in a variety of national journals, and is the author of two full-length collections, *Nome Poems* (West End Press, 2000) and *To Live on this Earth (West End Press, 2002)*. His five CDs, *A Week in Eek, Burnt Down House, Music Party, All Originals, All Traditionals,* and *Fiddling Poets on Parade,* mix poetry with old-time fiddle and banjo.

A college professor for several years, Waldman has been a poet-in-the-schools in over twenty states, and has performed in hundreds of venues, large and small, from the Kennedy Center Millennium Stage in Washington, D.C., to the Hopson Middle School in Barrow, Alaska. He holds a MFA in Creative Writing from the University of Alaska in Fairbanks. And all that stuff about the airplane crash is true.

For more information:
www.kenwaldman.com

Colophon

This first edition of *The Secret Visitor's Guide*, by Ken Waldman, has been printed on 70 pound paper containing fifty percent recycled fiber. Book and section titles have been set in Whiffy type; poem titles in Souvenir type; the text was set in a contemporary version of Classic Bodoni. The font was originally designed by 18th century Italian punch-cutter and typographer, Giambattista Bodoni, press director for the Duke of Parma. All Wings Press books are designed and produced by Bryce Milligan.

Wings Press was founded in 1975 by Joanie Whitebird and Joseph F. Lomax as "an informal association of artists and cultural mythologists dedicated to the preservation of the literature of the nation of Texas." The publisher/editor since 1995, Milligan is honored to carry on and expand that mission to include the finest in American writing. To that end, we at Wings Press publish multicultural books, chapbooks, CDs and broadsides that enlighten the human spirit and enliven the mind. We know well that writing is a transformational art form capable of changing the world by allowing us to glimpse something of each other's souls.

Wings Press uses as much recycled material as possible, from the paper on which the books are printed to the boxes in which they are shipped.